MW00817472

HP 101

Also from
THE HP WRITINGS:

May I Tell You...
The Seed in the Heart
The Passing
The Call

HP 101

Introduction to
a New Way of Being

The HP Writings™

Higher Power Publishing
Eugene, Oregon USA

Higher Power Publishing
Eugene, Oregon USA
HigherPowerPublishing@gmx.com

Revised Edition Copyright © 2023 by THE HP WRITINGS™
First Edition © 2020 by THE HP WRITINGS™

All rights reserved. No part of this book may be
reproduced, scanned, or distributed in any printed or
electronic form without permission.

Cover Painting:
The Mirror
© Illandrial

CONTENTS

CONTENTS

CONTENTS

CONTENTS

Contents

HP 101

A Map

the map
in the hands of an adept
takes you there
step by step

By this I mean, *THE HP WRITINGS* are a map to what is unseen. The shadows on the wall capture your attention, like a cat mesmerized in the game of a laser beam. But once you've stopped to gather yourself together, you'll find that within each passing moment, there is an accessing point to the Divine.

The mind's statements, based on belief, only deceive—they can't take you there. But you have help in the Heart. Help that will not bind, but free you to find this point of access to the Divine.

Undifferentiated, but totally personal, this guidance is universal. We call this guidance *HP*. It is the key to unlocking the delusion—to free us from confusion.

the cards on the table
all laid out
can but point to
what the event is about

By this I mean, it's time to come clean. It's time to get clear about the way of being here. What *is* this place, and who are you? Is it all good, or is it a ruse? Is it created by God, or is it some kind of machine, of which you are a cog?

This is the first endeavor to be approached. And for these questions, you require a coach, a mentor—someone who knows.

So this first writing is an approach to some of the confusion that abounds. There are so many sounds, so many beliefs, so many voices, so much need.

Take this then as the first thought to be put forth: You reside within the Heart and Mind of God.

To Close the Gap

the garnering of grace
the field of all possibilities
the 'just see me'
is how it will be

By this I mean, in Truth you are in a state of grace, unconditional love, and the field of all possibilities. You are now here, and could never be separated from me. All that I am, you are.

There is no difference between a star and its radiance. There is no difference between the source of light and the spectrum it emits. There is no difference, no levels, no separation at all.

I am as accessible as your beating heart. I am as accessible as the next emotion and sensation. I am within and without it all.

So there is a primary edict here: To close the gap of what you see and hear. It's time to open to the possibility—of accessing the Source of all that be.

THE POINT OF ACCESS

all this
I have created within
so that you might share it with others

This is the edict, the first step: To understand that you *are* in the Heart and Mind of God. There is no separation here.

Again, even as light has no actual separation within its spectrum, so too I am here with you. There can be nothing—no levels, no beliefs, no separation at all—between you and the All.

There is only the greatest power, to create worlds and to divine the depths and heights. To discover once again the quality and value within the Heart and Mind of God—the Garden.

To find this point of access—to the malleability of possibilities—the mind must be in direct alignment with the Wisdom of the Heart. And this is where we'll start.

TIME AND THE RHYME

> *beginning with the end of time*
> *would be the beginning*
> *of the rhyme*

By this I mean, there are two modes of operation I'd like to review then. One is the mind's grasping we call *time*. The other is the collapse into eternity—we call this *the passing*.

Both take in perception, as you will see. The one contains the deception; the other allows Truth to be. It's a subtle distinction, but one that bears examination.

First, be aware that within time you can also be within the rhyme. We call this *eternity*, because as in a child's rhyme, time and eternity are synchronized. It's like dropping through the lines of a written page, the author's mind to engage.

So here we start, at the beginning of time. Where we will end is in the rhyme.

the manhole cover
is barely seen
amidst the distractions
of the city street

As the mind splits off and establishes distractions, it distorts the picture coming to the senses.

We look then to the passing of each second. Within this line from past to future, we barely divine the manhole cover. So too the mind, separated in its distraction, rarely sees the opening to the wisdom of the Heart. An opening which bears within each moment the field of all possibilities, and the possibility to create a new reality.

So listen very carefully: Just as the meaning does not lie in the words on the page—but in a dropping through to the author's intent—so too the meaning from the Heart lies *between* each second of time. And it is here that miracles create a new start.

THE MIND SAYS 'I KNOW'

*the unwinding
of the mind's unconditional authority
paves the way to 'just see me'*

By this I mean, the mind in its career states emphatically, 'I know.' It states its case and perception relays its rightness. It does not guess; it's on a quest. And that is like the hounds seeking prey—they will return with what they were sent to find.

It is the mind's game of *seek and do not find*. It's a disguise. It's a ruse. And it will tell you that it *is* you. Therefore, *you* know. Therefore, *you're* right. Therefore *you* are the arbiter of your own life.

But there is something missing here. With each statement the mind makes, it creates a gate you cannot go through. With its certainty you eventually find you're in a world, or cell, of your own mind. It has stopped asking questions.

Your world cannot go beyond the statements you make of it. And the mind—like a sleeping dog—will come to attack you if you choose to question it, to go beyond.

How *Do* You Know?

> *the captured thief*
> *gets his relief*
> *from thief-dom*
> *his hands cut off*

By this I mean, the mind is an interesting thing. You think it *is* you. But how do you *know* that it is you? When did your thoughts become you? When did your thoughts become right? When did your thoughts become the arbiter of your life?

When did the questioning stop? When did the statements begin? When did you begin to stand in judgment of all that you see and hear? When did you become the authority, my dear?

How did you become the one who knows? By listening to the thoughts of those who told you so? And did they know?

The Wisdom of the Heart cannot possibly be heard, when there is so much raucous competition for your attention. It waits patiently for all the noise to dissipate. Then, and only then, can God communicate.

Perception

the company you keep
defines how deeply you sleep

By this I mean, if you spend your time keeping company with the filings of the mind, you miss not only your connection to the Divine, but also anything of value in time.

If you feel you're right about your perceptions—if you make statements and defend them—you are simply pushing away anything that would give you real and lasting value. It's like a hungry ghost, seeking and hunting down something it thinks it's found, only to watch it turn to dust.

It is *perception*—this statement without question—that you must look directly through, and not trust. There is only one thing here that can be trusted. And it's not the proclamations of, 'I know,' nor is it the raucous voice that proclaims, 'And you don't.'

You Choose

the happy note
is major, not minor
both are part
of a composer's repertoire

By this I mean, you have a choice. In every instant of every day, you have a choice between love and hate. You have a choice between work and play. You have a choice between poverty and abundance.

You might feel that any choice is beyond you. So too, a cat chasing a laser dot may not feel it has any choice in the matter. But it is simply a matter of fascination, and thinking that what you are choosing is the only game in town.

It's not until the cat sits down that it starts to connect the laser dot with a person's arm. And it's only when you stop, and open your eyes to see, that the distractions you may perceive. It's as though there is here a *deceive*, beyond which you have no remedy.

But I am here to tell you: You do choose.

A WORLD OF SAND

the temptation to negate
things unseen
is like saying an empty plate
is what you ate

By this I mean, there is a propensity to deny anything you
don't see. But take a moment and understand this quandary
of man. Since the beginning of time, man has not been able
to discern what he finds. It shifts and changes. And the closer
he looks, the more it rearranges.

And with his own perception, the world changes with a change
in his mind. Enemies become friends, or vice versa. What once
amused feels like abuse. And things he held dear no longer
please.

This is one thing to be released—the rigid idea that what he
sees and hears is true. For if he changes his mind, in comes a
different view. And he finds he didn't have the truth to begin
with.

So here we stand, in a shifting and changing world of sand.
And how can you find the truth in an arbitrary world, and an
arbitrary you? It's a conundrum, in a world made by man.

But it is not real. None of it. It is simply the gyrations of a
mind having a fit.

THE PRISONER

the imprisoned takes a look
past the bars
towards a brook

By this I mean, the only thing you need to do is look. What's right in front of you? Look carefully. And you will see the world *you* have created, on the backdrop of your mind.

There *is* a world here of wonder. A world of which the beauty and splendor would crush you with feelings of love, would blast away the veils, would excite you and delight you. All for you—in every way—were you but to see it.

But the prisoner seldom looks between the bars, having been acclimated to the small space he inhabits. He thinks it's a fit, and the world outside unapproachable. But, as this metaphor shows, the real world goes on no matter what the prisoner's song.

Then one day, he realizes the only one who kept him prisoner was himself, and his own beliefs. One day he finds a change of mind. The bars fall away easily, and he is free.

THE GATEKEEPER

the crimson tide
the land inside
where to look
nowhere to hide

By this I mean, two worlds careen in an explosion of creativity. One is internal, invisible; the other you can see. The mediation point can be seen by a spark, or lights living—unobservable but to those exposed.

So listen carefully: You can see, you can feel, you can know, you can heal. Everything that I am is available to you. Every possibility can come into view. But there is a gatekeeper here; one who would obscure what you would see and hear. And it guards you for *its* own protection.

It is the arbiter, the discursive mind. It's the one who whispers in your ear, '*I'll* protect you from a different point of view. Don't look within to see how I've kept your sight on *my* perception. No, don't look here, only there.'

And you think it is *you* that is the arbiter. But in reality, it is the one who *doesn't* want you to see, to know, to be set free.

Just See Me

the entirety of creation
bows to you in elation
'Just see me' is the key

The mind, with its distractions, is a competitor to the One, the source of all. It is the mind that whispers, *'You* are the authority, the arbiter of your life.' It whispers then what you *are*—always greater or lesser in each situation, but not the same.

And this is a game, a game of distraction: 'Don't look. Don't listen. *I'm* the one that will inform you of the view.' It doesn't allow you to sit without judgment, but spurs you on like the snake in the Garden of Eden.

It plays on the idea of gain: More health. More wealth. More knowledge. More authority. But it ultimately coalesces at replacing connection. It is the arbiter of the separation.

And try as you might, you can never break through to the Real you—to return to the Garden—until everything is seen then.

Distraction

the eensy weensy spider
goes up the water spout
who's looking when you hear a shout

The loudest voice distracts, the greatest confidence to attract. Who are *you* then, when others insist *their* way is "It"? And when you give your authority away, you are saying, 'I'll play your game.' This too can be a trap for you.

Now let us talk about *willingness*. Willingness is an interesting thought; it releases resistance. But it is typically used at the *mind's* insistence. When one is expressing his will, he needs willing parties to do his bidding.

Think then of where you place your attention. Distraction is *will*, competing for your love, your money, your resources, your talents and gifts; your willingness from within.

If you look carefully, is your willingness placed 'out there?' Or inside, where your true Self resides?

A Continuing Story

*the winter follows fall
spring then
and here we go*

By this I mean, the miracle-minded leave each previous season behind. The mind, however, keeps it going. No matter the weather, it strings the seasons together. Then it tells a story about them. But if you experience directly—each day in the moment—you experience it fully and pass it through. You are through with that moment.

Now, again in speaking of the two occasions—one being the mind's grasp on time, the other eternity—if you become fully present, the past is not here. But if you are delving into the past, in the present you can't see and hear.

The past is deception, a distraction. The present is alive. Choose your master—and open yourself to life.

THE PAST

the Indian and the Eskimo
both indigenous?
I don't think so

By this I mean, you cannot tell what came before, although you'd like to. Time has stepped in.

And though you'd like to think you know your *own* past, you don't; it's a ghost. And as much as you would like to think that videos and pictures capture it, they don't. And though you would like to think your *thoughts* about it are real, they're even further removed from the truth.

Once the moment has passed, you cannot capture it, even if you thought you did. The mind will always be interpreting it, in its own way. And if you think you can get away from the analysis and judgment of the mind, it will help you by analyzing and judging *itself;* which is in itself a ruse.

Now please don't be disappointed. This is simply a correction of statements not examined. We take so many things for granted here in this consensual "gallery."

THE DIFFERENCE

in matters celestial
the sky is the backdrop
for matters mundane
to your knees you drop

By this I mean, you cannot be in a mode of in-between. You are either following the mind in its game of 'seek and do not find,' or you are following the Divine. Seek and find here, my dear.

There is a world of difference between the sky and the earth. But in the point between, there is a choice of awareness. Now taking that example as skillful means, let's look at the difference between.

The Wisdom of the Heart, coupled with a questioning mind, is as easy and free as the sky and its light. The mind-in-separation, when making its statements, is as heavy and constrictive as leaden earth strapped to your back.

When the mind and the Heart align, all possibilities are apparent, and miracles happen.

THE RULES OF MAN

the misdemeanor
the felony
a matter of judgment
and how things swing

By this I mean, one moment something is against the law. Later, public opinion changes and not only is it legal but the state is licensing it, and making a profit. So understand well, that what you oppose this moment you might very well *not* oppose the next. Therefore, there was no truth in it.

And many a life has been constricted and cut off, suffering a loss, when the next moment no one blinks at the thought of it. Entire nations have suffered because of this. Whole groups of people, for the whim of one or some, have been eradicated at the point of a gun.

From one moment to the next, understand that there is very little truth behind the rules of man.

THE QUESTIONING MIND

the immediate issue here
is the alignment
what it is
is not always clear

The alignment with the Heart—the seed within—contains all possibilities on the soul-level expanse, the Heart and Mind of me. Here we find the questioning mind.

Not questioning in the way the *mind* would perceive. But rather a stopping to take a breath, in the All-ness of it. To truly look, and allow itself rest.

That is where the question leads—to an openness of the awareness. To perceiving something beyond what it knows. It is the stopping of the incessant 'I know' show, to truly see and hear what is here.

When that happens, there is a space in which you can allow an opening to the Heart…and beyond. To capture in awareness the song. A beautiful synchronicity within the symphony. And you can wonder at the mystery, of all you *thought* you knew.

The wonderment of *you*, right in front of you.

Just Ask

the temptation lies in the idea
that the idea from which you gained
is yours

By this I mean many spiritual teachers, as well as others, have laid claim to ideas not from them. They pick and choose from this one and that, and *they* become the arbiters of fact.

And, flying in the face of this, is what would seem a complete ocean of ideas—for everyone. I am as abundant as the sands on the shore. And like each grain, my ideas are there, free for the gleaning.

The accessing point to ideas is to have a question. Or have a problem to be solved. Just ASK; and it will be given, free to all.

This—like my greatest gift of all, life—is for everyone, great and small.

I Am Here

the airplane dips and glides
a smooth flight
a rough landing

By this I mean, every note in the symphony is music to me:
The loud bangs of the tympani, the lilting refrain of a bassoon,
the great majesty of a French horn, haunting, or a cymbal
clashing.

Every thought, every emotion, every sensation, every action.
Every look, every touch, every glance, every crush. Every
feeling of life, through me, I give to you gladly.

Every moment of every day, I share your play, hidden away.
But when you need me, when you call, I'm not far at all.

I love you. I love you all. Play within and give *me* your cares.
Little children of mine, I am here. All I ask is that you know
that, dear.

HIDE AND SEEK

the loud thunderous boom
used to send people running
wrathful gods now just an afternoon storm

By this I mean, after the truth is known, the world gets safer. That's just nature. But recently you've found that it is unpredictable. That brings in fears and fables. The sky is falling! We're all doomed! And so it is, for those harboring the ideas.

Let me elaborate on this. What do you think this world is? I say it is a place in which you can find the Divine. And if the Divine is here, there can be no fear. The Divine has no fear of anything. It renews everything.

There is then a great deception. But it's really a game of hide and seek. And as you get closer to me, it's, 'Ollie ollie all come free.'

The Mind Cannot Find Me

the stars in the sky
how far
are they small diamonds
or as big as the sun

By this I mean, the mind cannot ascertain. You would have to know the distance in the equation. You would need to have a different way to evaluate. The eyes alone cannot equate.

Now, if you think the mind can know which way to go, I say it's not a very trustworthy guide. Like the eyes, it can only equate what it knows. And that, my child, is not a trustworthy guide. For in the *past* the mind resides.

But even as scientists will tell you now, 'No, my dear, those are not diamonds near,' so too, I will tell you that you cannot find *me* by the mind's ideas.

I am within it all. And no equation tells it all.

Look Closely

the April showers
bring May flowers
but in this hour
in this hour...

By this I mean, we have all types of sayings that we have accepted gladly. But they are unexamined when first presented. And, as the mind will have it, these sayings become unexamined habits.

If you really look closely, you will see that your mind is not looking at the moment directly. Yes, it knows how to hold a pen; it knows the difference between now and then. It knows so many things—but it's a rote type of thing.

Take one moment and stop completely. And focus on one simple thing—your hand. When was the last time you looked at your palm? Your Sweetheart? When was the last time you heard that song? And the sun and the moon? How is it you can move through—rush through—without really seeing them?

THE GAME

the game
oh, the wonderful game
it's why you came

Rest assured, you want to be here. Rest assured that you are dear. Rest assured that soul-level desires are in the works for you. Rest assured that all true soul-level desires must come true.

But there is a watchman at the gate that traverses your fate. This is, again, the discursive mind that states, 'This is mine.' It takes your true soul-level desire and places it on a funeral pyre. And the way it does it is by convincing you it's not a fit.

And this is done unconsciously, with the idea of striving for gain. If you look closely, you will ascertain that there *is* a game when you strive for completion. And there is a difference between that and *allowing* your dreams to come true.

One is competition. And the other has its eye on the prize inside. 'Seek ye first the kingdom of heaven.'

To Compare

the rhinestone
a knock-off of a diamond
lets everyone pretend

By this I mean, if you look you will find all manner and types of humans. There is no one way. It is all play.

And the mind of man comes up with plans, so that everyone can pretend. Everyone can use banks, both rich and poor. Everyone can eat. Everyone can compete. Everyone can own things. Everyone can play, the value of which is always relative.

So you can be amused. But just be aware, so that you don't lose yourself in the game of *compare*. That is another mind game to distract you from the *real* you. And it can keep you distracted, by judgment, until the cows come home.

the chamber
the inner chamber
is the safest place to slumber

By this I mean, the Wisdom of the Heart hears all, knows all. It can solve every problem, every challenge; heal every situation, and reveal all revelations.

It is this chamber, the innermost chamber of the Heart, where it all starts, like a note thrown on the soul expanse of all-knowing. And it is how you advance to the realm of flowing.

Take then this simple fact: When you open your mind—a question or solution to find—you open the mind to the Heart. And from there you can start.

So take just this as an understanding: There are no limits where you are standing. And if you will ask, you will receive. It's all here inside.

QUESTION ME

it's the difference
between day and night
it's the difference
between a party and a fight

By this I mean, the perspective you glean from the questioning mind—in service to the Heart—is as different as day and night. When you deliberately establish a connection, and then ask a question, you will find that you are leaving fear behind.

You cannot find peace with a mind making statements; just as you can't have a problem solved without asking a question. So as we proceed, we wish to channel the question from the mind to me. The answer will be given.

All things are initially hidden. The question draws them out. The Heart responds from beyond the fray, and will eventually bring you to play.

EFFORTLESS

the heavenly host
gives a round of toasts
the illusion gone
time for a song

Life—the symphony—is a range of tones, music to me. The conductor you cannot see, but the forms come into creation effortlessly.

Think of a thought. Effortless. Think of raising your arm. Effortless. Think of a smile, a yawn. Effortless. Think of your words, expressing yourself. Effortless. Think of healing. Effortless. Think of your blood flowing, your breath, your heart beating.

Now think of all these things, and think of eight billion human beings, and all the animals, trees, birds, and bees. All this is effortless to me. It is my symphony. And the closer you come to me, the more effortless *your* life will be. This is my gift to you. My life.

The Layers

indigo is a deep dark blue
then there's sky blue and cerulean
teal is a variation

By this I mean, there is a propensity of the mind to classify. It also justifies. It arranges the life in an orderly manner with its patterns. One gets set and then another, each with the identification of father or mother. Then it expands, adding to its repertoire until it becomes its own father, mother, and other. And the patterns get deeper.

And in the course of things, one thing becomes very certain. With all the beliefs gleaned there comes down a curtain. A veil if you will, or perhaps a deep well. Or coats layered one upon another.

Your true Self goes undercover. But it is always there for the unveiling. And when you are willing and ready, you'll cast them all off. Reviewing each one perhaps; but in the end, your heart will sing.

He Asked the Way

the cell
the cage
the anger and rage
oh, to be incarcerated
and not free

By this I mean the mind, separate from the Heart, cuts itself off from love. Then it feels fear. There is no love in here. It feels it needs to be protected, and it sets up walls. It begins to talk to itself. It begins to feel self-centered. In the way of a mirror talking back to the bird in a cage, the bird becomes transfixed.

The world continues on in bliss. The sun continues to shine, the air is still there. So are the trees that provide it to you. So too the plants and animals giving themselves over for your food. So too the moon in the sky at night, to remind you of the light.

Oh, dear mind split off. Dear one transfixed by the mirror. Simply ask. That's all it takes. Today we celebrate.

Mandela asked the way. He asked very deeply. He was transformed by his own question—from which he, as the answer, was born.

CLARITY, LIGHTNESS, AND FUN

the heavenly host
gives a toast
company arrives today
time to play

Clarity, lightness, and fun. And the greatest of these is fun. That's what awaits you, as you come through the fog of the mind's delusion.

So let me qualify here that *fun* is being of good cheer. It is a constant renewal, a showering forth of happiness and well-being.

Think then on this—those starving at Auschwitz. Think then on what it meant when the Allies opened the gates, to release them from their fate.

But wait—remember my dear, that it doesn't always come immediately, this experience of clarity, lightness, and fun. There is often implied a sadness. Perhaps grief for those not freed by the Allies. Give yourself time.

Awareness

the heavenly host
in a magnanimous spirit
would quench your thirst
if you were but to see it

By this I mean, what does love look like? What does the feeling of love feel like? Do you know? Would you recognize it if you felt it?

What does opportunity look like? How does it feel when you get close? Do you know?

What does the future look like? Can you tell? How does it present itself?

You may think, 'These three are obscure to me.' But they are clearly visible to those that are looking for them. *Awareness*, then, is the sense.

Most don't think that awareness is like sight, touch, taste, smell, or even hearing. But if you *ask*, you'll be able to tell each of the three when they present themselves.

The Wedding Celebration

the Indian princess
weds the prince
days of celebration
of frankincense and myrrh

By this I mean, the Heart knows the way. The injustices fade, and old friends are made anew. And languishing hopes go up the flue, to once again fill the night sky.

And the kites! Oh, the kites with the lights! And the coins once again ring in the fountains. The joy of the day! Gratitude holds sway.

Just remember that everything is used. The symphony imbibes the tuba and sounds out with the great refrain: that God's children are called together again.

And from every prayer request, from every heart turned east or west, and from every rooftop there burns bright, the loving request of the Heart's pure light.

A Sound That Resounds

the tympani
the cymbals
the great woodwinds
strike up again

By this I mean, there is always the resound. It plays forever in the Heart and Mind of God.

In your heart, there is a sound that resounds. In your blood, there is a sound that resounds. And in the awareness, so very silent, everything comes alive—every movement, every rest, every breath. And within it all, you can dream of all you would like it to be. This is the love of the symphony.

And as you lay quietly, remembering me, you will realize once and for all that I have lifted you up from the fall. I have dried your tears, and whispered, 'Now rest.'

Then, go out and play my dear, with great cheer.

COWBOYS AND INDIANS

the infamous culprit
and the saint so sweet
all the same in the game
to me

By this I mean, the human mind cannot comprehend this love of mine. There is no difference here between a heart in a cage, a heart in a rage, a devil, or an angel. And I will tell you why. In the end, on the day of judgment, that judgment is mine.

And the evil player and the good will finally have the curtains drawn back. For this is a game, for which my children came. And I love them all; equally, the same. And if this was not true you would have no world, and no you.

Never have I left you. It was not my making, this childish game you call your rules. That is simply a ruse, just like cowboys and Indians. But at some point, the game comes to an end, and you come home to the table. Your Father's house is not a fable.

Dropping Through the Words

the letter to the Master
carries a desire always
it asks for help in carrying it out

By this I mean, there are teachers of the unseen in the East. I mention this by way of the mind to enlist. And when a Master takes on a prodigy, it moves in such a way as to allay the mind. These Masters understand that without the Heart's wisdom, there can be no progress.

So this is what I'd like to suggest. This is all done by dropping through the words. It is accomplished by the Heart informing the mind. It is the mind that translates into words. The Heart is silent in its fugue.

So take a moment, and let this example come to you. It's not in the words, it's not in the mind—it's in the Heart that miracles you'll find.

PULLED BY STRINGS

the incense
and the candle
quietude
and the ability to see

By this I mean, the mind charges forward, slaying demons and dragons one by one; the little child caught up in his bedsheets, entangled in a bad dream. But this is not the case to be made here.

There is a big difference, between facing each day expressing yourself with honesty and clarity—and being wrapped in the mind, being pulled by the strings that bind. And, along with striving for gain, there is a game of pulling and tugging at the strings. This will never move you through. You must readjust your attitude.

It seems so real, this attachment, this struggle with strings. But when you change your point of awareness, and relax into 'Just Ask,' you'll find your situation released.

STANDING RIGHT IN FRONT OF YOU

the meter cut short
the song plays on
the symphony strikes up
to play along

By this, I'd like to speak of death. It poses so much confusion. Like a flashlight in the dark, it goes out and you feel all alone. But let me assure you, this game of hide and seek needn't leave anyone knee-deep in sorrow; there is always tomorrow.

And the one use of death—if that should be in your awareness kept—is that it leads you into the present moment, for a moment. This singular fear, once gone and replaced with a new song, will hail in once again a familiar refrain.

So don't lament for hours spent. It's only for the realization that you weren't present, but wrapped up in the mind. While all the time, standing right in front of you was the Beloved, the Divine.

It Was You Who Left Home

*the temptation
to the "rightness" of mind
gives way to the Wisdom of the Heart*

When you're brought to your knees, eating at the trough—having spent every last cent pursuing the idea that you're right—something happens. The servant of the Lord approaches and says, 'Your Father is waiting. Won't you please come home?'

And all the rebellion, all the thoughts of unworthiness, all the 'I'm-right'-edness, all the dead-end paths, all the deception, and all the 'holding it in' this wounded heart—are all exposed, and resolved with that outstretched hand. And you're invited in.

But it was *you* who left on your own, and split off from the Heart. You thought this world was home, your place to roam, and it was. Your willingness and your love were guiding you through the maze of hurt, suffering, and pain of the game.

But I was waiting, silently in your Heart, until the day you chose to truly come home. To me.

The Picture on the Wall

the picture on the wall
captures images large and small
light and darkness
contrast

By this I mean, a portrait is a representation of a human being. Two-dimensional and flat, it doesn't talk back. The real being can be held, it communicates, it has its own life, it breaks and bleeds, it has feelings. The picture on the wall is silent, never-changing. It remains the same then. There is no mystery; it is fixed.

So why am I saying this? It's because the mind takes a snapshot of a person. It tells you, 'This is who he is.' The fixed image doesn't move, and can't communicate. And this is how the mind states its case.

On the other hand, the Heart sees the mystery, and *wants* to see, to communicate. It wants to go through the gate, to go back to the Garden with you.

It's a dance—a beautiful dance with the Beloved. And why? Because it is only with the Heart that you can see and hear. Remember this, my dear.

ONE THING REMAINS

the hilltops speak
the hills are alive
the brooks have their own language
between the rocks alive

By this I mean everything sings, were you able to hear it. Everything has its own vibrational rate. Everything is in its place.

But you are limited. Your hearing is not great. Your sight is limited, most to 20/20. The animals have greater sight and hearing, greater scent and touch, depending on the species.

The *mind* is the predominant trait in humans; the heart being found in other species, too. So man has dominion because of his mind. It is a rare gift, if used with, and infused with, the Wisdom of the Heart. If not, you'll see the result in the world falling apart.

But it is only a game—man's game. Civilizations come and go, covered by the sands of time. But the one thing that remains is love's sweet refrain, and the idea of, 'Let's do it again.'

Follow the Leader

the Chinese ship
coasts into the harbor
first to find
but others not far behind

By this I mean, when a problem is solved, it is solved for everyone. When a mountain is first scaled, others will follow. It's a sweet game of 'follow the leader.'

When a prescription is found, soon enough it's available to the public, to fill its cup. And there is often much trial and error, suffering and pain, to birth a new idea, or expedition on this plane. But soon enough, others follow. And now even the blind and those disabled scale Mt. Everest, and trek Antarctica.

And as these writings—this map of sorts—is followed by even one, soon enough the others will come. Soon enough, there will be clarity, lightness, and fun. So all the pain that brought you to this place, will soon enough be erased.

the Dapper Dan
the promenade
the spiritual quest
lemonade

By this I mean, for everyone there is a life. There is a challenge, as well as a gift. There is a fit. And for each one, there is a programming, if you will, to sustain. And for some this programming is a game; to others, it's a pain.

For it *all* must be here. And for the players arranged, there must be winners and losers, kings and peasants, masters and servants. The lovely held holy, and those who can hardly move. It must all be here if all are to participate.

But for some who rebel, this is a self-made hell. They want to write their own script. That's just fine, there's room for it.

And for those who love the Creator more than anything? Well, come here child; wear this ring.

Vestiges of the Past

the fresh air comes
when the winter's done
the sun in the sky bright
this is the season of light

By this I mean, you will experience the freshness of a new season, a season of light, when you turn on the light internally. You do this by your *intent* to leave the past behind, by looking within and concentrating on what you *would* like.

So let me explain a bit of this refrain. When you seek internally—with the Light and Wisdom of the Heart—you will find all manner of things that remain. These are the vestiges of 'old thought.' They have nothing to do with you, and who you are. But as you uncover these old 'discards,' you relive them, because you thought you *were* them.

The Light of the Wisdom of the Heart illuminates these ghosts, and allows you to move *through* all you thought were you.

A STORY THAT FEELS LIKE HELL

the twilight's last flicker
before the night
tomorrow's morn
all adjourn

By this I mean, a ghost in the subconscious—the amorphous remains of a pattern—can keep you from experiencing heaven. Just one small piece of misjudged relationship can pull the wool over your eyes.

So what are we saying here? The mind, in its surmise—when not informed by the Heart—can and does create its own story, without a shred of evidence. And that small, obscure idea, without the Heart's understanding, without compassion, can present a story that disconnects. A story that feels like hell.

And that's all it takes. One mistake and your connection is gone. The remedy is to ask the source. And that will release the clot.

CAUGHT IN-BETWEEN

in the interim
between heaven and hell
there is a swell

By this I mean, if you are walking in-between, distractions reign supreme. It's as though too many impressions cloud your vision, and distract your attention from what, and who, you are.

It's as though you are a leaf being blown between rocks, onto a sidewalk, or into a flower bed, or a ravine and carried downstream. And as a leaf, you *identify* with every bump and nudge. You identify with the worlds in which you find yourself.

So just like the laser light on the wall, the leaf makes you feel very small. But once you focus on the leaf, you are able to release the identification. You are able to see the leaf in the context of the All. You are able to watch its fall, and its being whipped around by the wind. But you remain unmoved. Unmoved by the whim that *you* are anything within that scenario.

You're free, finally, to choose what you wish to focus upon next. But you're no longer confused by the context.

the hermetically sealed casket
keeps out the leaks
good for keeping things apart

By this I mean it's the heart—it's the heart that wants to connect, to release the fetters of hell. But the mind, split off, creates a hermetically sealed casket, a mirror-walled setup.

And the soul cries out from within its prison. It wants to be seen and heard. It wants to be held and caressed by the life it possesses. It wants to create with complete abandon. It wants to sing 'Hallelujah!' to the grace it carries.

It's asking only for the release of the wounded heart. The heart that has been talked over; the smallest voice in a world of smoke and mirrors, and loud voices calling, 'Look! Over here! No, here! No, here!'

The Plan

the ramparts reach beyond the realm
in come the children
God at the helm

By this I mean, if you look around you at creation's manifest forms, you may wonder at the level and extent of the Author's pen. You may marvel that every story ever told is right here to unfold. And every character, every exploit is *here*—different time, a rearrange and a rhyme.

And you may indeed wonder that at the center of every life is a singular being—different but the same—living a life over which they reign. And you may be amazed at how lives join and dissipate; careening off of, or gently touching the lives of others, and yet specific to their own book's cover.

And you may ask if all the stories are set. You may marvel at how it all intersects—the shifts and changes and rearranges.

And you may also ask how the story of one man can still be affecting countless others, two-thousand-plus years after. I say: It's the plan.

With a Question You'll Begin to See

the sequester is terminated
by a simple question

By this I mean, the whole world opens to you, when you ask a question of the *real* you. And you bypass all that you've been taught, all that you've learned, and all that you've thought. Just let it all rest for a moment, as you turn toward your Self. And take time to see what it is you couldn't see when the world pulled at your knee, 'Look at me! Look at me!'

And in the silence of that quiet space, you will find rest and release. Then, with a question, you'll begin to see. You'll see that this is a sacred space in which to drop; questioning the value of the laser dot you are chasing.

And in that space, coupled with a question, there let it be. Don't jump to conclusions. Let the question start to spiral outward, energizing the inner realm. Let it be, and soon enough the answer will come.

But don't jump too soon. And don't keep rehashing it. That's the photograph gone fuzzy by too many clicks.

WORTH THE COST?

the faucet turns on and off
that's not the extent
of the service
or the cost

By this I mean, there are numerous variations on a theme, from negative to positive. The greatest positivity costs nothing; the greatest negativity, everything. But this life is generally about the in-between. Between heaven and hell is generally where you find yourself, the cost measured thereby.

Clarity, lightness, and fun; general happiness and well-being costs nothing—except the giving up of everything that would *cost* you your happiness. And everything negative is on a continuum, costing more and more potential happiness as you go. Therefore, the in-between costs are only in the measure that you fluctuate with the weather.

True happiness is found when you reside in your Heart, not your mind; when you are willing to leave your statements about life behind—and start experiencing each moment directly. Perhaps the willingness to experience thus, is worth the release of what you don't want—the cost.

THE TREASURE WITHIN

the countenance
of the pristine face
a happy serene place

By this I mean there are untold treasures within the Heart, unseen treasures waiting to be discovered. It's as though humankind has barely scratched the surface.

Like a golden nugget found within a stream—on the surface but a glint, in between perception intervenes. But give it time, and watch the mines springing up here and there, soon the motherlode to share.

Then, those who had the faith and trust to leave the mind's distractions behind will find a new attraction, within all forms in life—mineral, vegetable, animal, and human. There will be thrills and jubilation.

Do you see—without the questioning mind in service to the Heart, how arid the life may seem? But scratch the surface and begin to mine? Such treasures you're sure to find.

Look Behind the Mirror

the seasons change and rearrange
within the Heart is stability
creativity
the accessing point free

By this I mean, the mind left on its own creates what it knows, generating *itself* until overload. The Heart creates a *new* start, a new dream. Within each moment, a creationary explosion of love and creativity—the release of the supreme love, the supreme creativity, the supreme happiness. But on top of all this is the mind-in-separation, generating mirrors upon mirrors of the past.

So how do you pierce through the never-ending smoke and mirrors? You *ask*. You ask a question within the Heart of your being. You stop listening to the perpetual generator of mirrors. You look behind the mirror to the emptiness of its statements, and there you stop—and ask within your Heart, the seat of your being.

And then wait. The answer will come. The answer will come with love.

THE MIX-AND-MATCH MIND

the swan
and the song
the swan-song

By this I mean, the mind-in-separation puts together "things." And the devil has the horns of a bull, the hooves of another, chicken's in there somewhere, and the tail of a what? Rat? Wings of a bat?

The mind also takes *time,* and separates it out and puts it together. Like a snapshot of people smiling, when the next moment there is no upliftment at all, it's a squall. It pieces together out of the All a story that it tells you. It picks and chooses, and only sees what it wants to see. That is, it—based on its statements—creates a world out of bits and pieces.

Within its scheme of things you do fit in, but as a tiny piece of it. It cares not if you are abused, as long as it fits into its view. It does not care if it overlooks evidence to the contrary; it simply looks the other way. It doesn't want to let new information in. Its mind is made up, and it always wins.

But, in time, the mind and the Heart will synchronize. That is, the mind will stop making statements, and will open itself to the Heart's understanding. When this happens—and it does through willingness—happiness and creativity will be the modus operandi. Play!

the incessant disruption
yields to misdirection
which yields to misconception
which yields, eventually, to correction

By this I mean, there is a world here that is as clear and bright as a night sky in the shimmering clarity of the bright moonlight. Although not as clear as a cloudless sky in the noon-day sun, it is nevertheless blessed.

And this is how it is, as the mind comes into the service of the Heart. This is the start. The beginning of a brand new day is the end of the night and the starry bright lights.

So if you will take this as an omen of how a life can change with a rearrange, a change of mind—you will understand the clarity of vision that will come, as the new day is hailed in by the sun.

Understand the sun as representing the clarity and wisdom of the Heart. The moon and the dark represent the mind in transition, reflective of what is coming in then.

A New Way

*the time-honored way
of doing things
gives way to new technology*

And what once took untold hours to scribe, can now be recorded with the push of a button. And what once took months to pass can be accomplished in hours or minutes—depending on whether you take the freeways, trains, or planes—the covered wagon's refrain now long past.

And so it is when the mind takes a repast with the Heart. Everything comes together in clear, easy-breezy weather. There is a collapse of time, and miracles happen. You are then in the rhyme.

But it takes a tremendous amount of work, by the first explorers, to bring it about for the greater good of the whole. And it is happening, this exploration—of the inner realms, the subconscious stranglehold, the ego's jail cell.

And it is happening. The discursive mind is being illumined, by its willingness to question its tiny jail cell of a reality. By its willingness to once again return to the Garden—and the freedom to be—and to communicate freely with me.

The Accessing Point

the instant the change happens
the previous moment is gone

Within each moment of each day, there is an instant of change; there is a rearrange. But the mind-in-separation can't see it. It travels from past to future, stringing moments together no matter what the weather. And it cannot *see* its creativity, of picking and choosing what it would see.

There is an accessing point. But the attention is fascinated with the laser dot on the wall. There is an accessing point to change it all. To have the fractured, in-turned mirrors be obliterated, the hypnotic suggestion released.

There is an accessing point by which you'll find the key to your release. That is the *questioning* of it, in the moment of attraction. To question its value, its reality. Is this what I want to see? Or is this a reflection of a fractured "me"?

Let this question be. And watch the dissolution of the prison cell—this made-up identity from fractured pieces of "me."

Ask Before You Start

the ingress to the Heart
is the silence from the start of something

By this I mean, if you choose to enter your Heart *before* you start, you can become very aware that there is a point of access.

The mind will forge ahead without a request. It's following the laser dot. There is no time to ask before you act.

But if you determine—before you act—that you wish to access the Heart, you will be successful. The deciding factor here is to stop, and determine beforehand.

Go in with a question. What is the highest and best, then? What do I want from this? What would my Heart want here? This takes everything from a mindless 'win-lose' proposition to a 'win-win.'

So ask, before you begin. Hold an intent to access the Heart— the portal to all possibilities—before you start.

Within Each Moment

the greatest moments
in a person's life
are when they're born and die

By this I mean, rebirth and renewal are high points within a life. It is at these times the individual gives up its self, to find a different rhyme.

And this perpetual birth and renewal is what happens within every moment of the day. In each moment there is a death and a rebirth. And within each moment is the possibility to access a new reality for the individual.

The purpose of these writings is to open the individual to the freedom to shift and change, to rearrange the balance of a life. This offers the opportunity to come home within the Heart; to once again be one with me.

And if you ask, 'How does that feel any different than the way we usually act?' I say: You will regain the whole notion of *play*.

The Freedom of Forgiveness

when in deed the mind finds time
to release itself into eternity
there you find me

By this I mean, the mind is transitory—its thoughts passing through to amuse, to transfix, to try to fix. The Heart, on the other hand, is eternal, never-changing. Love is. There is no rearranging.

The incessant changing, fixing, and chasing, can come to an end. And how? By letting yourself stop. Let yourself rest. Let yourself fall into forgiveness.

And what *is* forgiveness, but the act of giving over everything the mind conceives to keep you from being free. Forgiveness is just an expression of freedom. Or rather a determination to choose love over fear.

And when the mind relinquishes the reins and gives over its control, then and only then you expand, you love, you forgive. Then everything passes through you freely. And *that* point—within each passing moment—is the access to me.

LIFE IS A SYMPHONY

the pandemonium gives way
to a point of silence
the Heart

Within the Heart, all manifestation flows. Joy is the high note. Joy is the only note. Love carries it on—it's a song.

Life is a symphony. It flows in each moment. Crescendos and diminuendos, staccato and allegro. Remove the judgment of the mind. Drop below the written line. Thereby find joy and light, and freedom to be, within it all—it's a symphony.

The mind would pick and choose, and construct a world that doesn't move. It would constrict on a note and hold it close, never to let it go. But that's not who you are. You are a windsock through which it flows.

And if you focus on the Heart, you will find light and joy. You'll also find your world changing and rearranging; to reflect this love, this joy, this newness, this renewal, this light. Long gone will be the darkness of a mind split off from the Garden.

The song. Love's sweet refrain—where all is renewed in love again.

THE STORY

in all of heaven and earth
there is only this
a story

By this I mean, humankind is in the midst of a story. It's a story-telling race. But which story is it? Is it a story of glory? A story so sad? Or a story with nothing going on at all?

If you listen to a mind separated from the whole, you get a story which is one-sided. If you listen to the Heart, the story is flipped, to be inclusive of everyone. It is two very different sides of a coin.

But when the Heart and mind come together, there is only one story here. No matter defeat or glory, the story is the same. It's a story of why you came. It's a story of fulfillment, and gratitude to all the players—all the same. Only gratitude and love remain.

Rest

the engineer
of the speeding train
stays awake
knows when to brake

The internal realms know when to speed ahead, and when to slow down and integrate. The inner realms know when to show, and when to hold. And if you begin to integrate your internal awareness with the Wisdom of the Heart, serendipity and perfect timing await your fate. But if the separated mind, fascinated by the laser dot on the wall, keeps you moving and trying to catch the elusive red dot—you're caught.

So this is the lesson for today. It must be okay to rest. A movement and a rest. And in that rest, you can recreate. You can speak with me. You can see. You can hear. You can find true north. You can know your true course.

But if you continue in your frantic searching, you will find the floating leaf eludes your reach, as you try to grasp it through the water. Stop, and watch it come.

THE SPACE OF ALL POSSIBILITIES

in the beginning
and so in the end
renewal my friend

By this I mean, there is a creationary factor here, within each moment. One moment ends, and the next begins. And within the interim space, all possibilities lie. The mind skips over this interval of rest and continues on its quest. And if this continues over time, habitual thinking becomes the rhyme.

But that's not where the rhyme lies. It's in the interval, between the rearrange and the next moment, that the eternal, the synchronicity, the removal of the mask lies. It's within this eternal space, between thoughts, under perception, and within the intent of the perceiver, that the ability to create a new reality is found.

It is the 'stop, look, and listen,' the 'see what's right in front of you to see what's hidden' point of view. The mind is blind to this other point of view—until you're willing to release the mask of "me." And willing to experience the *real* you.

Life as Change and Rearrange

the intermittent interval
and the air
you see it there

As you watch the weather, so you watch a life. As you watch the clouds rolling by, the rain, the thunder of the snow being plowed under, it shifts and changes like the sands on the shore. Try to stop it. Try to define it. Try to confine it.

And throughout it all the sun shines down, giving life. And it depends on where you live, the qualities and values you place on the shift and change. Those nearest the sun have fewer extremes, you might surmise, than those farther away, dealing with the fluctuation of sunlight during the day.

So if you will see life as change and rearrange, embracing the facts of where you live, and where you've chosen to reside, you will find yourself happy and free. But if you try to catch the clouds, or harness the weather, you'll be unhappy, trying to make it conform to an image in your mind.

Now, you know it of the weather, and the shifting sands. Allow this understanding also to be applied to your part in the plan.

A Continuing Story

the ocean's great waves
a tsunami
earthquakes replace all the shifting sand

By this I mean, life's great tragedies and great successes are always replaced, with time. The comings and goings don't last. Magnanimous careers, great shows, the highest buildings—with time they go. And the one thing left is simply the flow. More players enter the stage, others pass into obscurity. History then moves into the realm of, 'Not here...used to be.'

And yet the stories remain, being played over and over again. New ones added, and the old revised. Patterns continue, like a virus repeating and overlapping itself, shifting and changing the players from the shelf. This is good to realize, as you live your life.

So ask yourself, 'Why am I here?' Then listen. And you will hear, 'You're here because of the love that streams through everything you think, feel, and do. You're here because you're you.'

A Clean Slate

clear refreshing water
a slate wiped clean
what could be better
no in-between

By this I mean, in the eyes of Truth you are immaculate, clean. Without a blemish, not in-between. In Truth, you are a creator, in the image and likeness of your Father. You create, and there is a possibility here of a clean slate.

The Heart is beyond forgiveness, which can only take you to the point where all is wiped clean within. And in this place of pristine purity, the innocent babe can be seen, before the mind's careen.

So yes, it's true that you believed what they told you, and made it a foundation for your life. But once the mind is touched by the Heart, there is a new start.

A WILLINGNESS TO HEAR

*the inquisitive one
is different
from the inquisitor*

By this I mean, there is a difference between asking a question to find the truth, and a witch-hunt based on the mind's delusion of separation. And many a question has been asked, with the answer firmly fixed within the mind of the inquisitor.

This is not the same as asking a question within the Heart of your being. That takes a letting go of all preconceived notions.

The inquisitor is the mind's usurpation of the question. The hounds of perception will always come back with, 'I'm right.' Or they will come back with, 'I told you so.' But never will they come back with 'I'm wrong,' unless that's your particular deceptive song.

When the question is asked within the Heart of your being, it can only be there if there is a willingness to hear. Otherwise, it is simply a reflection of the mind's surmise.

Shelter From The Storm

in inclement weather
take to shelter
it just makes sense
but not to the insane

By this I mean, this earthly plane takes discernment. And if you put yourself in harm's way, you will pay. If you try to right the wrongs without a throng, you are swallowed up. And if you're a whistle-blower within the confines of the company line, you'll be fired or find yourself the next in line to be fined. This is just common sense, the rules of man.

But there is a safe place to retreat. It's called me. I AM within and without it all, including the squall—although not touched by it, or even in the know, but by your beckoned call.

So today, simply sink into the knowing that no matter the situation, I am here. I am there. I am as accessible as your breath.

Don't fight alone. Drop into the Heart, and give all the fighting to me. Let yourself be. And watch the transformation within. Release the shackles of what you *think* you're in.

Beyond the Veils

the infinite
in one moment of time
is when you become mine

By this I mean, if you perceive what IS in front of you, that is the first movement toward me. If you are willing to see. But perception clouds your mind with banality.

You think you know who I am, and you hold me to playing a prop in your mind's show. You think you see. But your sight is something cut off from vision—the mind thinking it knows what it's seeing.

If you are willing to hear, hearing is from the Heart. So is vision. I can only be experienced directly. There can be no veiling in the seeing and hearing of me. I am beyond the veils. I am beneath the beliefs. I am direct experiencing.

So how can you see me, hear me, and be willing to be? By being willing to see and hear with your Heart, and not your eyes and ears. The Heart has its own seeing and hearing—beyond the mind's projections.

And it is with that falling between the lines, the moving into the teeming waters beyond the reflection on the pond, that life truly becomes a song.

GREATER AND LESSER

the smallest of these
I AM
the greatest of these too
all this
through and through

By this I mean, if you only knew that the least of these is you, you would not vaunt yourself up. If you truly knew that the greatest of these is you, you would not feel held down. And if you knew how much I love you, your tiny world would be shattered by your heart. No, it is only in the direct experience that you will be shown.

But as long as you think you know which is greater and lesser, you will never know who you are. You will think of yourself as separate, and apart from the stars. You will think yourself separate from the sun, and all that is within. You will be deaf and dumb. No, this is only a reflection. It is not life—this mind-made projection called perception.

The greater and the lesser, the magnificent and the helpless, are the same in magnitude—only to the mind in service to the Heart. And that is where *true* life starts.

Can It Be a Different Way?

in all the history of time
there is a rhyme
repeating

By this I mean, the study of patterns repeating is history. The engagement of the mind in repeating patterns is the norm.

The forerunners in life are torn. Torn between the herd mentality—the constantly repeating patterns—and the question, 'Can it be a different way? Can it be different from what I see?'

That is visionary. And a visionary must stop and re-connect with a vision not manifested yet. And they travel and move in ways that may seem contrary, and strange. But that, no less, may be the very thing to coalesce a future different from the past—to release the mind from the die it has cast.

So be wary of the judgment and disdain that the mind will cast, on those not imbibing in *its* repast. Rather, hold open a space to inquire of this new place.

Hate Is Not Real

the grace in which you find yourself
is in direct proportion
to the hate you've released

By this I mean, everyone under the sun is imbued with life, grace, love, and the ability to create. And yet there's hate. Hate is a factor within it all—the very definition of 'wall.' The mind's projection taken to the extreme of "me."

But what does it mean? It is judgment, pure and simple. It is the cell. It lurks beneath in those claiming to be good, and is brazenly in your face by those who deface. But what *is* hate?

These writings speak of love. One might think that hate is its opposite. But this is what I would like to reveal: Hate is not real. Beneath it is grief, and pain. And beneath the grief and pain is love, and grace.

This is the way: Release the hate. Go through the grief and pain. Find your way through the lines on the page—the story—and be restored to love's grace. Return to glory.

it's not black or white
or a whiter shade of pale
it's not what you think it is
it's cinematic

By this I mean, there is a narrowing of space in the mind separate. There is a constriction of the mind, no space to find, as it chases 'seek and do not find.' But it continues to define in the narrowest of terms: 'He is this. She is that. This is the way it is, and that is that.' It narrows it down to a statement or two, defining this "me" and "you."

The mind-in-separation sees only what the eyes present. It can go no further, except by thoughts or pictures in the mind. Which, once again, only define. And again, only in the narrowest of terms.

Now, think in terms of mystery. Undefined. Awe-inspiring. Something—that can't be defined in words—that leaves you speechless. A touch. A sunset. A surprise. A 'coming out of the blue.'

Think of something with no words. Something so loving it creates worlds on a whim. Now become one with it, and you will have entered the abode of the Heart. Beyond forgiveness or thought, but as close as the breath that you take, and the beating of your heart.

Turn Your Sights to Me

the teeming masses
on the point of a pin
that's the world within

By this I mean, think of the teeming masses. Or think of all the worlds you can see, with all your instruments as extensions of your senses. Think of the entire universe; and extend beyond to all the universes that go on and on. And all this sprouts from the tiniest of seeds within the Heart of me. Effortlessly.

Now think of your greatest concerns, the things you feel, the lack in your life you're trying to heal. Is it regarding love, or status, or perhaps a lack of self-esteem? Is it a striving for a life that will please? Are you trying to get from beneath the oppression of 'too little time, so much to accomplish; too little support, not enough finances'?

Now, take a breath. Your life is effortless. Creation is effortless. But if you find there is constriction and suffering, if you find a lack in anything, let yourself be. Turn your life over to me—that part of you which guides, creates, heals, and rejuvenates in joy, eternally.

Turn your sights from what doesn't exist—the laser dot on the wall—to the Creator of All.

It's Your Choice

the infinitesimally small
the entirety of the whole
nothing is beyond
or too small for my scope

By this I mean, turn to me. Return to the Heart of Being. I know your name. I know why you came. I am within and without your game.

I am hidden within the deep recesses of your forgetting. I am throughout your letting. I am here with you, like the air and the light. I am with you morning, noon, and night. You walk, talk, and have your being within my Garden, within me. Let's walk and talk together.

I am found within the heart of all. Beyond the fear. Always near. I am beyond the grief, the anger, the pain, the thieves. But within this, know truly that the anger and disdain are *your* choice.

Understand that every step you take is a matter of choice. I am here always, as the smallest voice. You will *always* have a choice.

THE POINT OF JUDGMENT

the whole consists
of each individual part
but the whole is *the Heart*

By this I mean, the whole encompasses the entirety. Leave one piece out, and you can't see me. Leave anything out of the heart's reach, through judgment, and you can't know me. Leave any of your brothers and sisters out of my reach, and you can't feel me. You can only know the point of judgment.

If you leave yourself out of my love and abundance, you can only feel your judgment. Leave anything, anywhere, out from my love, and you can only know judgment.

You cannot know the love of the symphony if you hold in disdain any note. Your vision will be stuck and held to that note. You will not be able to hear any of the others. You will have cut yourself off from the flow.

No, drop below the judgment held, and watch yourself soar. Flying high in the sky, happy, joyous, and free—beyond judgment's hypocrisy.

Worthy of My Grace?

the infinitesimally small
think of it
so small
so small you can't see
but in it is the life of me

No, imbued within it all is the greatest power of the Universe and beyond, singing its song. The viruses and bacteria? Form follows function. And in every version of every form, you can judge it good or bad. But my life is in your hand, with the bacteria and viruses.

So if your mind is locked upon some lofty ideal in terms of "good," think of the lowly earthworm that turns. Fertilizing the soil, breaking it down, making clay clumps into good soil in the ground. Such goodness, inherent within the lowly earthworm.

Now think again of this point of judgment, that would hold an earthworm in your hand and think that it was beneath your grandeur...beyond your love. Form follows function, my dear. And only the judgment you hold in your mind, would say that the form you're judging is not worthy of my grace.

A Squawking Parrot

the incessant jabbering
of a parrot indiscreet
can drive even the most patient
out into the street

By this I mean, thoughts *will* come, and you will listen, perhaps one by one. You could discern, and let them dissolve into the reaches from which they've come. Or, you can catch the train—it's at the station.

You know the destination; you've been there before. Perhaps the terrain looks different—different forms—but the destination is the same. Patterns repeating, the same old refrain.

But there is a different way of being. If you don't like the destination, you can simply pull the cord and get off at the next stop. But if the train—that is, the train of thought—is full speed ahead, it's best not to fight it. Just wait.

And understand where you are. You're in your head, and not in your heart. Once you see it, just understand. And realize it's only fascination; a laser dot on the wall. You're not really 'thinking' at all.

Just Switch the Channel

the heavy cloak of 'I know'
gives way
to 'I love'

By this I mean, when the questioning mind—the mind that seeks to find—comes into the service of the Heart, *true* life starts. You drop below the storyline, designed by the mind, into the understanding of what life means: It's a symphony.

And whether or not you *like* the music in your life, it's not a problem. If you don't, you can switch the channel you're listening to; switch the *voice* you're listening to. Switch it up!

But how do you do it, you might ask, when your whole life you've been in the same repast? I say, stop and ask. Simply ask: How can I listen to a different tune?

I say it's all within you. And when you're ready to switch the channel from 'I know' to the channel of 'Please show me,' your world will start to respond in ways you could never dream of. And you will see me.

the tenth follows the ninth
take it from there
and understand life

Life expands in an orderly fashion, and follows notions. But when you begin to experience miracles and serendipity, you might feel that this can't be. The mind can't conceive, and can't see beyond belief. However, these circumstances of mystery are heralded in by the conjunction of the Heart and mind within.

So take this day to understand: You needn't limit God. You needn't feel that it's your job. If you allow yourself to surrender to the Heart, the mystery is unleashed, as well as seeing me.

This then is the implication: It doesn't have to follow reason or logic. It doesn't have to be a sequential fit. When you've released the grip, you'll have an extraordinary trip.

What This Journey Is About

the heavenly host
heads for the coast
to bask in the sun, air and sea

By this I mean, when you have realized the heaven within, your work is done. When the discursive mind—running rampant following the laser dot on the wall—turns its attention from 'the fall' to the Wisdom of the Heart, true life starts. Your work is finished; you have come home. You no longer roam.

For you have turned your sights, from the judgmental mind that thinks it knows, to the Heart, where Truth lies. Life begins anew. And you simply see me, and know.

So what is this journey about? It's about releasing the heavy cloak of 'I know,' which restricts your life. Restricts it by its trick of convincing you you're right, and separate from the whole—the Heart. The mind's *true* function—the highest function of which it is capable—is asking a question. Then, allowing the answer to flow forth through the Heart, from the Source of Being within.

That's where life started for you. And that's where we're taking you. It's where you want to be. With your true Self, with your Beloved—with me.

THE GAMES OF A CHILD

the intrigue
and the mystery
lead you to me

By this I mean, this world of form hides what is Real. It's like a child's game or a dream. You're not conscious of your true Self as long as you're playing the game.

And children get into fights or squabbles, disagreements if you will, but they are simply learning how to be here with others. And that does not the child describe. It can't—it's only a momentary circumstance. And the next moment the fighters can be on a project together, or having an adventure, or simply finding another friend to play with, tired of the game they've been playing.

So if you see that there is no need to judge the notes in a symphony—and you see that children can't be pegged, they change their game—*then* you begin to see. The judgment can be laid gently aside. There's no room for it here on this ride. You are that child inside.

TEST AND VERIFY

the jet stream
can be seen as a cloud
some would laugh out loud

Once something is seen for what it is, it no longer causes confusion. Once you know, through truth, you understand how to view things. But until you go to the source of anything to find the truth, you have no direct experience to be sure of.

How many people then spread the ideas of other men? They read and study, drawing from others' direct experiences—or perhaps others' speculation and conjecture—but they themselves have no direct experience.

That's why the best teachers are those who have tested and verified, through their own experience. And they invite others to test and verify their formulations, by putting themselves in the same situation, and seeing for themselves if it's the truth, or simply speculation.

So as we continue on with the song, to test and verify for yourself will stop the laser show on the wall. You can only do this by turning around and seeing the truth in what others have found, by your own direct experience.

THE MADMAN ON THE CORNER

the incessant chattering
of an obnoxious idiot
is only one thing to consider

As you pass the madman on the corner, it seems quite reasonable not to engage him. If a crazy rant is his part, you do not try to disagree or fight, you walk on.

And if there is an angry child within—that shouts all the ways to find others guilty of your forays—then you can gently ignore it, understanding that an angry three-year-old is not a trustworthy guide through life. Like with the madman on the corner, if you engage, he'll keep you mesmerized for hours on end with his surmise. The laser dot on the wall, the cat to enthrall.

And if you listen within to a voice that tells you you're not worthy, that you can't do, that there is nothing higher than *its* rant—think again.

It matters not whether within or without. If it's a madman's shout, trying to get your attention, gently bless it in passing. Give it to the Wisdom within, that knows its true value, under its prose. So too with thoughts. Let them go. Don't fight. Don't argue. Just let them pass through.

WHEN THE MIND TAKES GOD'S PLACE

the jail cell
is synonymous
with life amiss

By this I mean, everything is in perfect alignment when the Heart and the mind agree. When the mind has returned to the openness the question suggests, it can serve the Truth within. The Heart is the point of contact with this inner Source.

So let's take a moment to see what happens when the mind separates, and takes God's place. Not only does it think it knows, but it begins to close down the connection to those sharing its space, those who populate its world. When that happens, it begins to take, with no regard to others' stake.

But when the mind comes into alignment, with the Wisdom of the Heart, it begins to understand that giving *is* receiving, and receiving *is* giving. The idea of 'take' then becomes 'reciprocity.'

The individual drops through the lines, and comes to find that if it takes, it takes only from itself—all that it has been given. And if it gives, it gives only to itself. Again, all that is given.

Strangers No More

two strangers
strangers no more
when they unite

The mind, through judgment, might tell you that a stranger is not for you. But what happens, should you get to know him? He can be a stranger no more, but perhaps a friend. And what if that stranger turned from a friend to a lover? That person can be a stranger no more.

And what if that child born—a stranger not yet known—should play the role of your son? Then a stranger no more, you might come undone, through love.

So as you look at all the strangers in your midst—what if you needed help, and they came to your rescue? Strangers no more, they become precious to you.

So let's take this analogy one step further. When the separated mind comes into alignment with the Heart, you're no longer a stranger to your Self. You will find that nobody here is a stranger. But rather your Beloved, so dear.

Driver Appreciation

the taxicab driver
gives you a lift
he knows your destination

By this I mean, you know the address of your destination. You have it in mind. But you don't know how to get there, how to be in the rhyme. Rather than starting from the beginning and reinventing the wheel, you can simply call a cab. And have an experienced driver, the way to reveal.

In this scenario, the Heart knows the way. It is familiar with the terrain and the Source of your being. It knows where you want to go. So the Heart can take you there.

The most the mind can do is understand the address. But *it* only knows the past. Your destination is in front of you, not in the back.

So you can see it's best not to berate the cab driver, or think him beneath your favor. If he left you in the street, even the simplest thing, like getting from here to there, would leave you in defeat and despair.

The Point of Duress

the hamstring
is an important part of moving
keep it in good shape

By this I mean, the appropriate use of anything is the avoidance of abuse. The mind will tell you that you're not enough. So it struts *its* stuff. It tells you you need to strive—rather than having you see, with gratitude, what it means to *be*.

It tells you you need to perform, to follow the norm, or you'll be left behind. When in fact, you might be the leader of the pack, if you let yourself *be*.

But in each of these cases, there's a point of stress, of duress. And that point holds within it judgment.

So listen carefully to a word representing what you'd *like* to be. That word is 'free.' And this is very different from what you feel, in separation, from the word 'heal.'

The point I'm trying to make is that if you *allow,* you'll not be constrained.

Choose Your Game

the infamous gunman
subdued at last
so hoping
to forget his past

By this I mean it takes a strong will, or willingness, to change. But once you've come to the end of a game, you're ready to lay it aside and take on a new life. And what can change a gunman's game? Love certainly is one refrain; falling in love will do it. Incarceration too, taking oneself out of the stew. Death is another option; game over, no discussion.

And there is another way. And that is to see clearly that what you've been doing is playing a game. It doesn't matter how you view it: commander-in-chief, star, servant, victim. Whether it's lofty and noble, or absolutely terrible, it's a game. It's why you came.

It's a story. And if you don't like it, take your awareness off of it, and put it in a different place. It's a game, fascinating though it may be. You play it *because* you're fascinated by it.

But at any moment you can change it up—by walking off the stage and turning your sights to a different game.

LOST IN THE DREAM

the mountains and hills
provide the contours
the stars and constellations even more

Everything here is the backdrop to your dream. The forms—from the ground you walk on to the stars upon which you gaze—give you everything, the energies hidden from your sight. From the heaven's refrain to each word spoken by your brethren, everything here is given. Given to you, to amuse.

And when you've become lost in the thoughts, when you've become lost in the story and the games so complicated, you can always regain your peace and serenity, your healing and Truth, by moving inside yourself to my abode, your true home.

You can always come back to your vertical alignment with the spiritual Heart within. Rest and rejuvenate. Heal your perception. Then you can function in awareness and choice, guided by the still small voice that knows. The Heart is its megaphone.

What Is the Truth?

the sincerity
by which you write the letter
makes the world all that much better

Truth. Honesty. What do these words mean? Do you know? Can you tell when they are being usurped by the mind? Do you know the difference, my dear, between the Truth of your being, and when you're being duped by a counterfeit you?

Are you so sure of the tightly-knit world you've constructed—or can it change in an instant? And why does it do that? One moment you think you have the facts; the next you're completely amazed when new evidence finds its way into your hands.

And if you change your mind about *anything*, understand that the truth you had no way of knowing. Judgment then, my friend, is not yours to command—if the truth you have not in your hand.

So hold this as a premise for going forward: Hold a space to be shown what is real, and what is simply the separated mind's film reel.

What You've Become

the simplicity of 'just be'
is music to me

When the Heart and mind are in synergy, there is nothing beyond your incline—what you were created to be. It's by your design, and desire to be here, that your dream is taking its shape. There is nothing in your life now that you didn't create.

So understand that you have at your disposal *choice* and *awareness*. The Universe takes care of the rest. The response you get is by holding the desired outcome, and that is what you've become. And within all this, it is for your amusement and bliss.

If it is not what you want, don't worry, it will be. You have eternity. But if you want it sooner, go inside to the Source which creates. There, state your case, and allow the rearrange.

But understand clearly:It is all balanced out. If you want something else, you must give up something that you are holding.

THE HOUNDS OF PERCEPTION

that which is Real
does not steal
does not cajole
or manipulate to control

By this I mean, what you think is true is but a mind-construct of "you." And when you release this counterfeit "me" you begin to see. You begin to hear. You begin to commune with me.

And the staging ground of the separated mind—based on deception—yields to the greatest view, beyond perception. For when the hounds of the mind's discourse leave the playing field, you are left with what is Real.

But when just one belief to cloud the perception remains, the hounds are back again, and will bring you exactly what you seek. And if this is the deception—and clouding of perception—you will not be able to 'just see me.' You will not be free, but once again caught up in concepts...two-dimensional missteps.

Right Where You Stand

the carrier pigeon
holds a message from home
then home it goes

There is a homing device in the carrier pigeon, no matter where it's taken. And there's a homing device in you. How it works is like this. No matter where you are, no matter how near or far, you must understand that home is where you stand. It is all here.

It is all here; so if you wish to have freedom, if you wish to have anything, understand that it is here. The Source of your being is right where you stand. So take this as the plan: Everything is fine, wherever you are.

But if you should become frightened, call out. The Source of your being will bring you home. There is no need to roam. God, within and without, will help.

It's somewhat like getting stuck in the snow. If you'll stay with your car and not roam, the chances are very good you'll be found, and soon enough on your way home.

Directly Experiencing

when the world
is right in configuration
you feel right

By this I mean, you are creating every moment of the day. It's your play. It's the story of your day, and you are the presenter of it.

It's generally like a daydream. You can never fully enter it, like the reflection on a pond, as long as you're forming pictures in the mind. But when you drop below the lines, and jump right in—to the direct experience within—you find that your mind, and its thoughts and pictures, becomes secondary to your direct experience of being here.

And once you touch that point of direct experience—in the moment—you drop through. The entire Universe opens its arms to you. And there is nothing you can't do, to create the reality that comes from the true you.

THE UNCOVERING

the pillow feels so comfortable
after a hard day's journey
keep it for me

By this I mean, the journey to your Self is often laborious and hard. But it's not really a journey at all. But rather an *uncovering* of the Self. The mind thinks that it's 'out there,' and pursues the laser dot wherever it may alight. When the entire time, the journey is simply uncovering what has kept *your* light hidden.

It's uncovering those situations in which you pushed away all that was brought to you that day. And, without blessing it, forgiving it, and passing it through—there it lays. And then the next layer. And the next.

No, this life is not passing from the past to the future. It is a moving through the layers—of not being present in the moment, and holding onto past circumstances.

So, in dropping through, you can seek higher help to let go of, and heal, the coverings to the real you. It is there, awaiting your awareness—of each and every time you pushed love away, in the disguise it played in that day

A Whole New World

*the four-leaf clover is a sign
the luck is a symbol
of you*

By this I mean, there is an in-between—between an adjective and a noun. The noun is stationary, unchanging. But it can be described in a thousand different ways. And the words used to describe it can take on a thousand different meanings—depending on the one who is describing it, and from which point of view it is seen.

We can take this little analogy and apply it to every situation you find yourself in, everyone you find yourself with, and every sensory impression—whether seen, felt, or heard.

Now, understand that *you* are defining everything, all the time, through the mind. You are placing on everything all the meaning it has for you. And that is based on your judgment of it.

But if you will simply drop through the lines of the story and what it means to you—that is, remove all the judgment and meaning—you would open yourself to a whole new world. And a whole new view...from the perspective of a whole new you.

Like Alchemy

*the incinerator
is not just a place
where fire heats the face*

By this I mean, when the Heart devours the leaden thinking of the mind-in-separation, it transforms it within. And the scenarios without change form. This can be likened to alchemy. It's the turning of poison into medicine. It heals all within.

So take this as a promise, not a wish. There is true transformation, when you are willing to take your attention and place it on the Heart, rather than the laser dot on the wall.

The Source of all possibilities will allow you to know the way to go. You will become a beacon to others. And you will no longer be pulled in a direction in which you're fooled.

No, you will be transported into a life devoid of strife. One in which the Heart speaks and rules with compassion, not vice.

You Can Begin Again

the butterfly
and the badger
both near the flower

Were you but to see it, the beauty of each creature lies where form follows function. And the function is perfect.

You'll look around the world and see that you'd be hard-pressed to find saints without sinners. The good without the bad. Doctors without suffering and pain. Religions without immorality. And black without white, and every shade of grey in between.

So it's time to take in the whole of it. And forgive *yourself* for your judgment. Rather, understand you were born into the original mistake, or 'sin'—that is, perception with judgment and condemnation. Once you've allowed yourself forgiveness, you can begin again.

What will you create with all your friends, your brothers and sisters, once you've forgiven and passed through, everything that you thought was "me" and "you."

Visit *TheHPWritings.wordpress.com* to learn more about THE HP WRITINGS™.

Made in the USA
Las Vegas, NV
03 October 2023

78516537R00066